AF483683

Grateful
by
Jacqueline Regano
Illustrated by
Pearly L.

This book is dedicated
to my daughter Brielle,
my husband Michael,
my family, and my friends.

I'm grateful for the sun,
which keeps our world
light and warm.

I'm grateful for the moon
and its beauty as the
ocean tides rise and fall.

I'm grateful for the Fall,
with its crisp air
and how the leaves are
changing colors all around.

I am grateful for pumpkins,
for they make life
so much fun!

I am grateful for apple-picking
and making fresh,
yummy apple pie.

I am grateful for the clouds;
I love how they change
into different shapes in the sky.

I am grateful for
my family,
I give them
lots of hugs!

I am grateful for my puppy;
she brings me so much
joy and **love!**

I am grateful for my friends
and for the laughter
and good times we share.

flour

I am grateful for my home
and how it is filled with warmth,
kindness, and care!

I am grateful for Thanksgiving,
with its yummy, big feast!

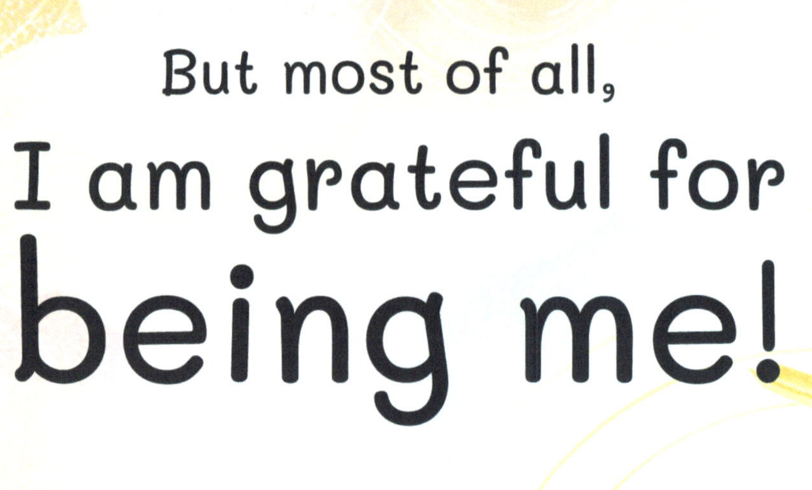

But most of all,
I am grateful for
being me!

What are you
grateful for?

Happy
Thanksgiving!

Other books by Jacqueline Regano together with Brielle Vivienne

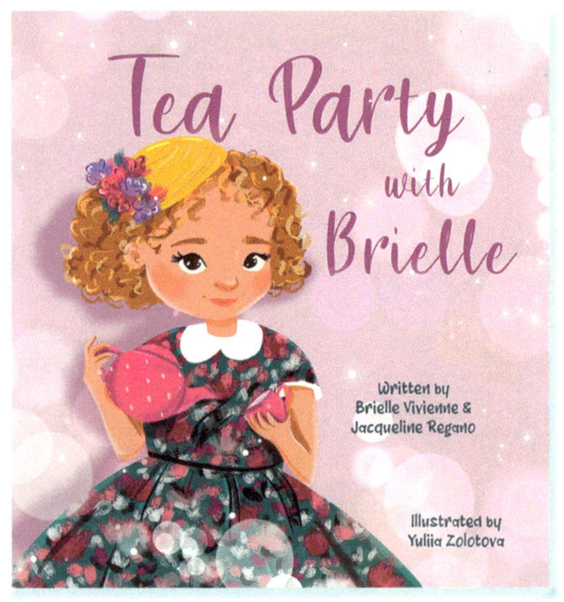

Tea Party with Brielle

https://www.amazon.com/Tea-Party-Brielle-Vivienne/dp/B09NRG4W12

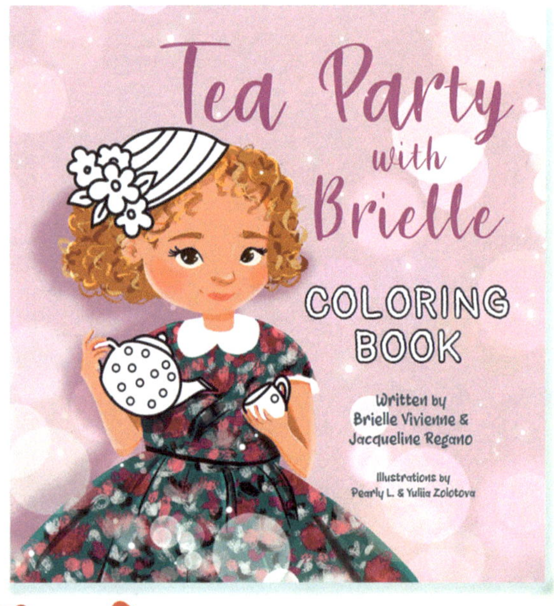

Tea Party with Brielle Coloring Book

https://www.amazon.com/Tea-Party-Brielle-Coloring-Book/dp/B09PM67CF8

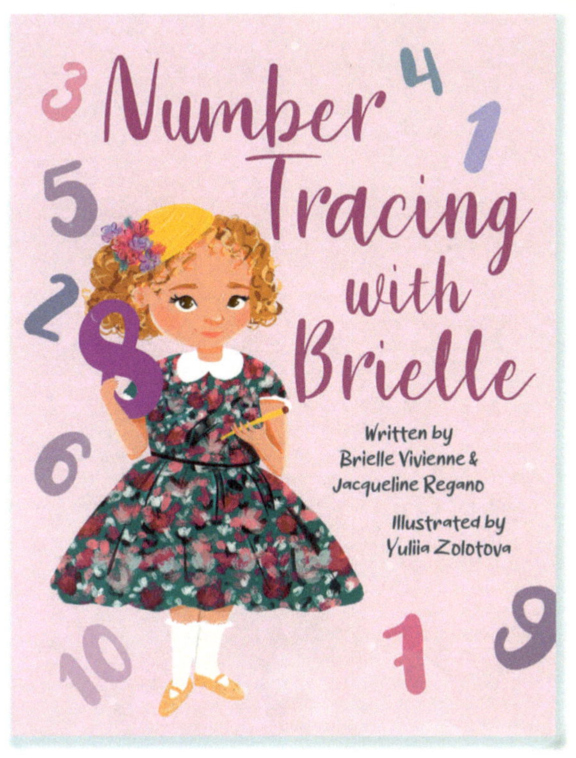

Number Tracing With Brielle

https://www.amazon.com/Number-Tracing-Brielle-Vivienne/dp/B0B2HQJH87

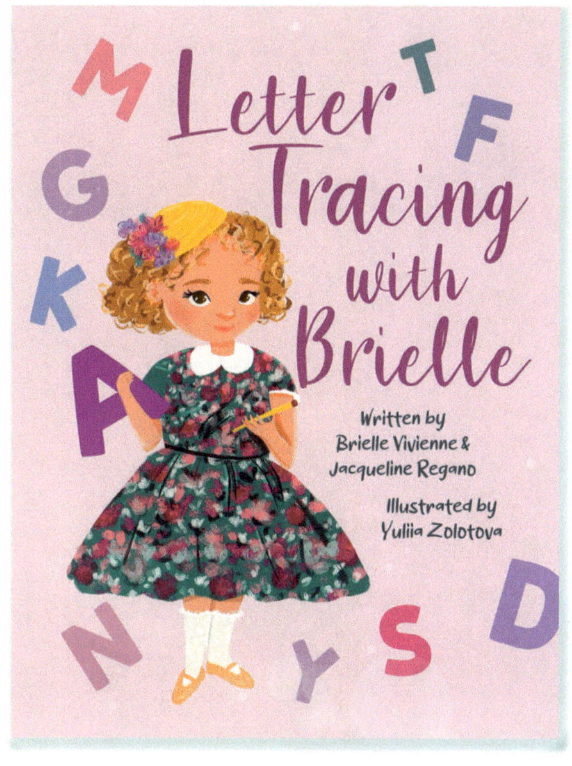

Letter Tracing With Brielle

https://www.amazon.com/Letter-Tracing-Brielle-Vivienne/dp/B0B3V4D8C1

Other books by Jacqueline Regano together with Brielle Vivienne

Valentine's Day Soirée with Brielle

www.amazon.com/Valentines-Day-Soiree-Brielle-Vivienne/dp/B0BVTHMZ8Q

Valentine's Day Soirée with Brielle Coloring Book

www.amazon.com/Valentines-Soiree-Brielle-Coloring-Book/dp/B0BYLN3H88

Join Brielle on her journey in hosting the perfect tea party!

www.briellevivienne.com

Tag Brielle on instagram @briellevivienne

Hashtag #teapartywithbrielle

Halloween with Brielle Coloring & Activity Book

https://www.amazon.com/Halloween
-Brielle-Coloring-Activity-Book/
dp/B0CHL7DJJJ

Other books by Jacqueline Regano

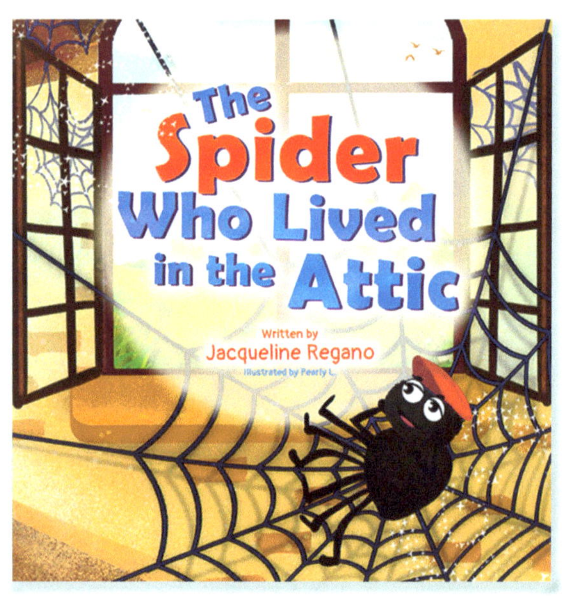

The Spider Who Lived in the Attic

https://www.amazon.com/Spider-Who-Lived-Attic/dp/B09M5LJV9G

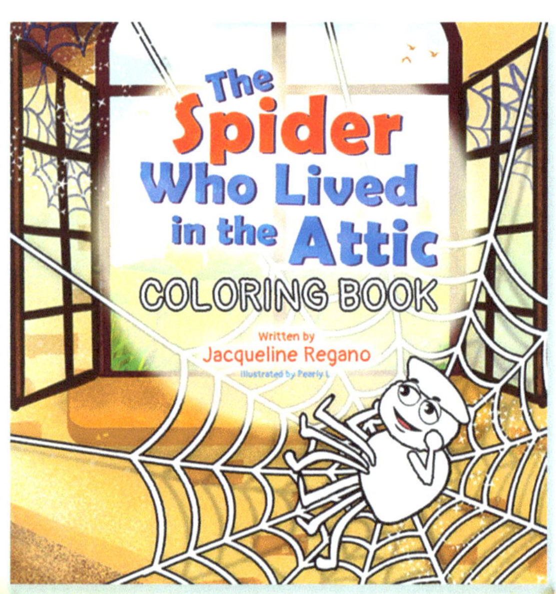

The Spider Who Lived in the Attic Coloring Book

https://www.amazon.com/Spider-Lived-Attic-Coloring-Book/dp/B09MGQF5MQ

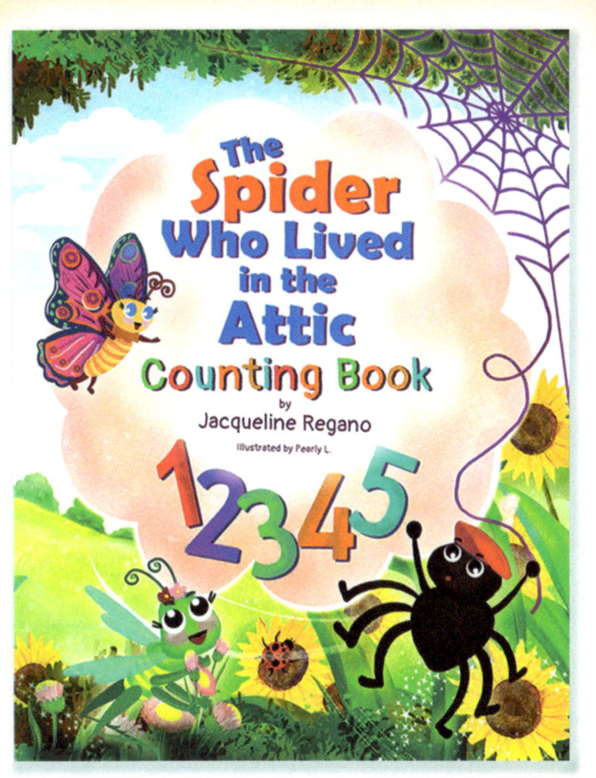

The Spider Who Lived in the Attic Counting Book

https://www.amazon.com/Spider-Lived-Attic-Counting-Book/dp/B09ZCSPNXF

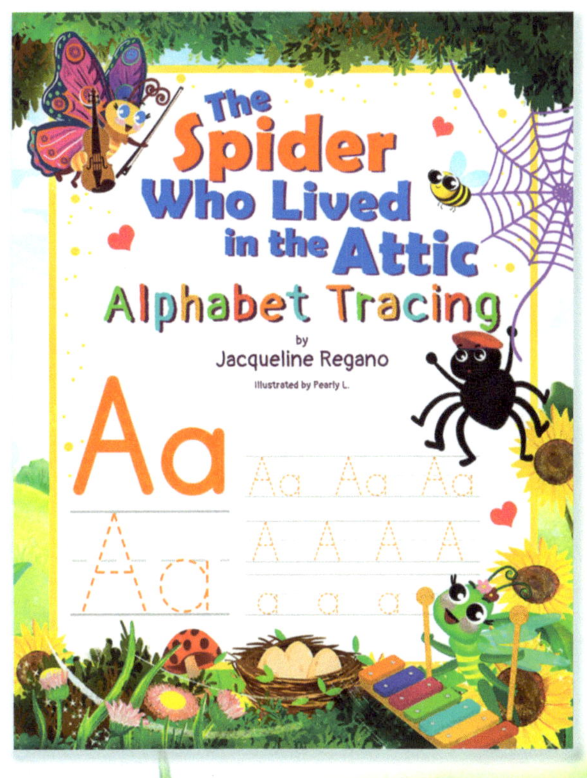

The Spider Who Lived in the Attic Alphabet Tracing

https://www.amazon.com/Spider-Lived-Attic-Alphabet-Tracing/dp/B0B1BCJWRY

Other books by Jacqueline Regano

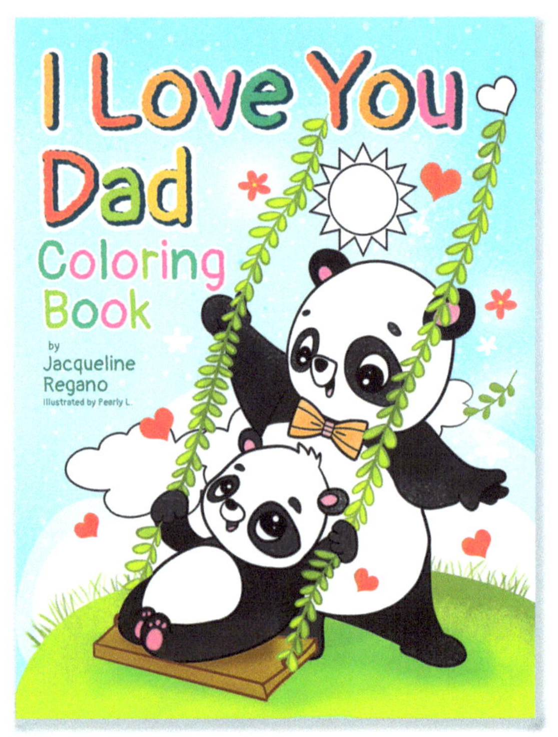

I Love You Dad Coloring Book

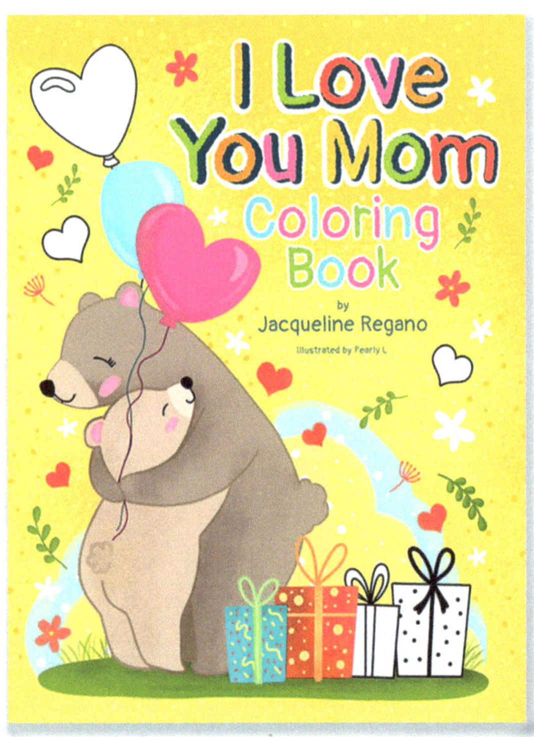

I Love You Mom Coloring Book

Dear Baby Journal

https://www.amazon.com/Dear-Baby-Journal
-Jacqueline-Regano/dp/B09RLWN8MX

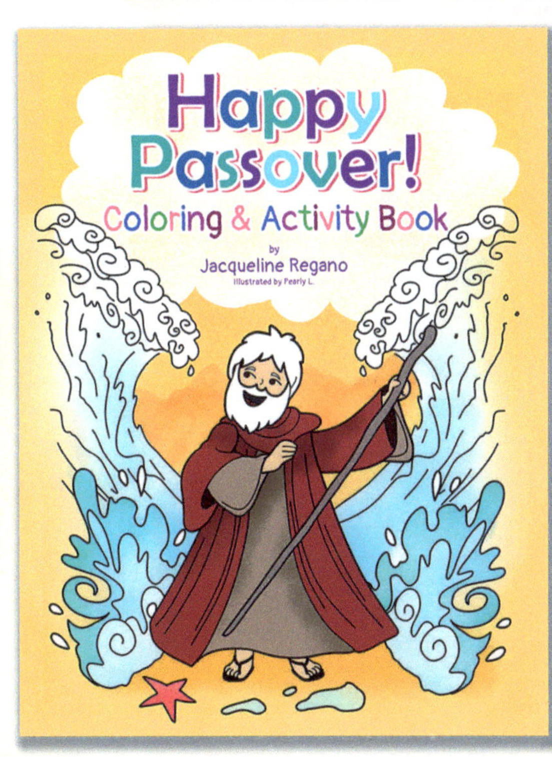

Happy Passover!
Coloring & Activity Book

https://www.amazon.com/Happy-Passover-
Coloring-Activity-Book/dp/B0BZFDFQKG/

Other books by Jacqueline Regano

Happy Easter Coloring & Activity Book

https://www.amazon.com/Happy-Easter-Coloring-Activity-Book/dp/B0C2XLLBXH

Happy Fourth of July History, Coloring & Activity Book

https://www.amazon.com/Happy-Easter-Coloring-Activity-Book/dp/B0C2XLLBXH